More Praise for *The Leader's Guide to Speaking with Presence*

"Baldoni's latest book capsules the basics of presenting with authenticity and confidence. The book delivers clear, concise, specific action items to add to any leader's personal success plan."

—**Dianna Booher,** author of *Creating Personal Presence: Look, Talk, Think, and Act Like a Leader* and *Communicate with Confidence!*

"No leader can accomplish much without the ability to bring people together for common cause. John Baldoni provides us with a road map with how leaders can use the power of their communication to connect with people authentically. *The Leader's Guide to Speaking with Presence* also provides practical advice on how to make your presentations sing and your messages resonate."

—**Mark Goulston, M.D.,** co-founder of Heartfelt Leadership and author of the best-selling book, *Just Listen*

"John Baldoni's new book, *The Leader's Guide to Speaking with Presence,* is full of well-honed, practical tips for successful public speaking that you can put to work right away. Keep this book handy and refer to it before you go on stage!"

—**Dr. Nick Morgan,** President, Public Words, Inc., and author of *Give Your Speech, Change the World*

Also by John Baldoni

The Leader's Pocket Guide: 101 Indispensable Tools, Tips, and Techniques for Any Situation (2012)

Lead with Purpose: Giving Your Organization a Reason to Believe in Itself (2011)

The AMA Handbook of Leadership (edited by Marshall Goldsmith, John Baldoni, and Sarah McArthur, 2010)

12 Steps to Power Presence: How to Assert Your Authority to Lead (2010)

Lead Your Boss: The Subtle Art of Managing Up (2009)

Lead by Example: 50 Ways Great Leaders Inspire Results (2008)

How Great Leaders Get Great Results (2006)

Great Motivation Secrets of Great Leaders (2005)

Great Communication Secrets of Great Leaders (2003)

180 Ways to Walk the Motivation Talk: Proven and Practical "How-To's" to Energize Everyone in Your Organization (coauthored with Eric Harvey, 2002)

Personal Leadership: Taking Control of Your Work Life (2001)

180 Ways to Walk the Leadership Talk: The "How To" Handbook for Leaders at All Levels (2000)

THE LEADER'S GUIDE TO SPEAKING WITH PRESENCE

How to Project Confidence, Conviction, and Authority

John Baldoni

AMACOM

AMERICAN MANAGEMENT ASSOCIATION

New York • Atlanta • Brussels • Chicago • Mexico City
San Francisco • Shanghai • Tokyo • Toronto • Washington, D.C.

Bulk discounts available. For details visit:
www.amacombooks.org/go/specialsales
Or contact special sales:
Phone: 800-250-5308
Email: specialsls@amanet.org
View all the AMACOM titles at: www.amacombooks.org
American Management Association: www.amanet.org

This publication is designed to provide accurate and authoritative information in regard to the subject matter covered. It is sold with the understanding that the publisher is not engaged in rendering legal, accounting, or other professional service. If legal advice or other expert assistance is required, the services of a competent professional person should be sought.

Library of Congress Cataloging-in-Publication Data

Baldoni, John.
    The leader's guide to speaking with presence : how to project confidence, conviction, and authority / John Baldoni.
        pages cm
        Includes index.
        ISBN 978-0-8144-3379-9 (pbk.) — ISBN 0-8144-3379-0 (pbk.)
    1. Leadership. 2. Public speaking. I. Title.
        HD57.7.B348944 2013
        658.4'52—dc23   2013014940

About AMA

American Management Association (www.amanet.org) is a world leader in talent development, advancing the skills of individuals to drive business success. Our mission is to support the goals of individuals and organizations through a complete range of products and services, including classroom and virtual seminars, webcasts, webinars, podcasts, conferences, corporate and government solutions, business books, and research. AMA's approach to improving performance combines experiential learning—learning through doing—with opportunities for ongoing professional growth at every step of one's career journey.

Printing number
10 9 8 7 6 5 4 3 2 1

To Kathleen Macdonald
Mentor • Colleague • Friend

CONTENTS

INTRODUCTION TO AUTHENTIC COMMUNICATION

What do people want most from leaders?

The real deal!

This is especially true when leaders open their mouths to speak. How they say it may be as important as what they say. Whether the person speaking is your boss or our president, we want to know that he or she knows we are listening and respects us for doing so.

Another word for this is authenticity.

We want people in charge to be honest and we want their words to ring with integrity. Never is this truer than when the leader is making a formal presentation or delivering a speech.

The words are crafted but the delivery must be authentic. It must reflect the honesty of the speaker, or something I like to call "leadership presence."

Leadership presence is the reflection of the leader's inner self. It should be the real deal. Presence, however, is not simply a sense of being; it is a determination of action. Leadership presence, as I wrote in *12 Steps to Power Presence*, is a form of "earned authority." Authority comes from the title of a leader, but it is earned by example.

A leader's job is to bring people together for a common purpose, so credibility is critical. That will only come when people trust their leader and want to follow his or her lead. Communication opens the door to understanding what the leader is and what he or she stands for.

The Leader's Guide to Speaking with Presence focuses on delivering the authentic message and doing it as a leader full of presence. There are chapters on crafting the presentation as well as on delivering it. I have also included information on using PowerPoint as a tool for enabling more authentic communications.

The Leader's Guide to Speaking with Presence is a result of lessons I have taught in my coaching practice, as well as tips I have learned from watching good speakers deliver. The handbook contains more than a hundred tips on what to do when speaking aloud, not simply from a stage or a podium but also when connecting one-on-one or in small groups.

Communication opens the door to authenticity. A leader's presence affirms that what the leader says is an indication of what he or she believes. And when we sense that the leader means well, we will lend the leader our ears and will be inclined to follow his or her leadership.

CHAPTER 1

THE SOUND OF YOUR
LEADERSHIP SPEECH

SOMETIMES REFLECTIONS on leadership lead us to unconventional places. Communication is central to a leader's ability to connect with others. One way leaders connect is through a formal presentation, that is, a speech. The types of speeches are infinite in style and content, but there is something more important than the style or content of a speech, and that is its ability to engage the heart and mind. And for that reason, I like to draw a parallel with something else that does the same, a piece of music.

Think of a speech as a piece of music. Like a piece of music, it has melody, harmony, and rhythm. Melody rises and lowers according to the words. Harmonies are facts and stories blended for meaning. And tempo, fast or slow, matches mood and meaning. Put more simply, every good speech must have its own signature, a rising and falling according to meaning and a tempo dictated by emphasis.

SCORING YOUR SPEECH

Understanding a speech as a score is not strictly an exercise in the arcane, so let me give some pointers that speech givers can learn from musicians and their scores.

- *Opening.* You want to grab the audience's attention. You want to state the purpose of your presentation, that is, what you are going to say and why you are here. Your opening emerges from your content. You may wish to pick out a point to emphasize and lead with it. Don't give away all the details, but you can, as with a musical phrase, give a foretaste of what's to come.

- *Pitch.* Up and down, crescendo and diminuendo, make music worth listening to. Your voice is your instrument. Sometimes you are loud, other times you are soft. Up and down. If it were all the same tone, it would become boring. Chant, be it Gregorian, Hebrew, or Buddhist, is delivered flatly. That's for spiritual effect. Speeches are a different matter; fluctuation in voice pulls the audience into what you are saying.

- *Rhythm.* Most importantly, your speech, like music, must be delivered with verve and pace. How often have you heard a piece of music played at the wrong tempo? It sounds awful. The notes may be correct, but if the tempo is off it sounds terrible. As someone who tried to play piano, I can attest to the power of rhythm. Listening to me try to play Gershwin was an exercise in "I ain't got rhythm." Pacing for a speech is the same. Monotone is deadly, be it slow or fast. We need variation.

- *Pause.* If you do nothing else in your next speech, pause. Nothing expresses presence like a purposeful pause. The adjective "purposeful" is essential. In music we call them rests or even pauses. They are noted for a reason. A pause could be for emphasis, or it could be for effect, or it could be for reflection. All pauses give your listeners time to reflect on what you are saying. Pauses are powerful.

◆ *Closing.* You want to leave them, as great musicians do, wanting more. You want to end on a high. As with your opening, your closing, be it a summary or a call to action, emerges from your content. So you could end with an upbeat and powerful closing, a mighty crescendo. Or you could close with a soft and intimate whisper. Whatever method you choose, make it memorable.

AN ART REDEEMED

Not all speeches will, or should, have all these elements. Some remarks are impromptu and spontaneous, though many a great speech giver, from Mark Twain to Winston Churchill, practiced long and hard on their "off the cuff" remarks. If you do have the opportunity to speak without prepared remarks, keep a couple of things in mind. First, open by acknowledging the audience. Second, vary your pitch; starting strong is fine, but ease up from time to time to give your audience a chance to digest your ideas.

Giving a speech is somewhat of a lost art, but like music, it is an art that can be quickly regained with rehearsal. Practice what you are going to say. Doing it in front of a mirror works fine for gauging your reactions and rehearsing your gestures.

One more pointer. It is not necessary to memorize what you are going to say. Musicians often have scores in front of them; they know the order of the notes as well as the time signature. The same applies to speaking. Go through your words thoroughly so you know what's coming next as well as the context of the words. When speakers stumble, it is less because of mispronunciation than because of forgetting the context, that is, forgetting why they are saying what they have written. This kind of brain-fade is not uncommon, but it comes from not paying attention or from focusing too closely on words rather than on sentences. Scan the sentence as you speak so you will emphasize key words. Otherwise you will sound like a first-grader reciting a poem about which he or she knows nothing or like a nonnative speaker sounding out words one by one.

Speech delivery, like playing an instrument, is an art that can be mastered; it simply takes a willingness to try and a commitment to speaking in public whenever you have the opportunity to do it.

ACTION STEPS

As you consider your next presentation, think:

- How will you open your presentation on a high note?

- Where might you pause for emphasis?

- How can you make time to rehearse your presentation?

- What are the high notes? What are your points of emphasis?

- What points might you emphasize with a pause?

- How will you close your presentation? Will you tell a story? Or will you issue a call to action?

CHAPTER 2

PRESENT AS A LEADER

HAVE YOU EVER SEEN an executive scurry across the stage with his head down, clutching a copy of his presentation, and begin speaking immediately upon reaching the podium? Such an executive resembles a mouse seeking shelter more than a leader about to deliver an important message! Yet we see this kind of behavior all too often. What the speaker has failed to do is acknowledge the audience. Worse, he has failed to demonstrate leadership, the kind that emerges from personal presence.

From my experience in working with executives, I find it is typically not the presenter's fault; she has not been schooled in basic presentation skills. For many people, speaking in front of a live audience can be so terrifying that their single overriding wish is to get it over with as quickly as possible. I teach the presenters with whom I work the art of the "metaphorical handshake," imagining introducing themselves to each person in the audience.

This is something you want to do when you take the stage to put the audience in a mood to listen to you. Even though they may be seated, they have a full agenda of things to think about from their work or home lives. As a leader, you cannot control what they are thinking, but you can, with your words and behavior, put people at ease and enable them to listen to you more attentively. That is a leadership statement. Here are three suggestions for accomplishing this:

1. *Make personal contact.* Look at your audience. Nod at people you know. Smile and relax your facial muscles. Some speakers like to wave at the audience, especially at people they recognize. Size up the audience as you reach the podium. Take a deep breath, pause, and look out at the group. Imagine you are a conductor. Your baton is your voice, but before you raise it, you wait for a beat or two.

2. *Acknowledge the audience.* Before you start speaking, comment on something that everyone in the audience may have in common. It may be the weather. It may be traffic. It may be a busy schedule. Put yourself in the audience's shoes and acknowledge their presence.

3. *Break the ice.* Effective presentations depend on connection. People want to know you, so you have to reveal yourself appropriately. No life stories please, but offer comments on the connection you feel to your audience. If you are comfortable telling a funny story, do so. If you are not, or if the mood is one of solemnity, then speak about the urgency of your message. These comments may seem ad lib, but you can script them in advance to deliver them as if they were off the cuff.

Of course, some skilled presenters actually do shake hands with audience members prior to taking the stage. They do it moments before the audience files in or as they take the stage. Politicians are adept at doing it. For a speaker, it is an energizing experience and also helps to break the ice with the audience.

Presenting effectively can be a huge challenge for many of us. But learning a few simple techniques about connecting with the audience can go a long way toward establishing a platform for confident delivery, and, more importantly, it can put the audience in a mood to listen to you. Most importantly, it affirms your leadership strengths and gives people a reason to follow your lead.[1]

ACTION STEPS

As you consider delivering your next presentation, think:

- What will you do to "make friends with the audience"?

- What steps will you take to put them at ease?

- What is a good way for you to "break the ice"? Will you use a story, a comment on the weather, or humor?

CHAPTER 3

MAKE THE AUDIENCE
FEEL WELCOME
(AND BANISH STAGE FRIGHT)

"ACCORDING TO MOST STUDIES, people's number one fear is public speaking. Number two is death," quipped comedian Jerry Seinfeld. "This means to the average person, if you go to a funeral, you're better off in the casket than doing the eulogy." Funny, yes, but for many people all too real.

Fear of speaking in public stems from many things, such as uncertainty about what to say, the perception that you might embarrass yourself, or even self-consciousness about how you will sound. These feelings stem from one thing: lack of self-confidence. How can you gain more self-confidence as a speaker? The same way (as the old joke goes) you get to Carnegie Hall: practice, practice, practice!

Good advice, but how do you get started? How do you get up the gumption to stand up and deliver? It is critical to adopt a different mindset. You need to project that sense of confidence even if you are not feeling it yet.

A crippling fear for some folks is the fear of making a mistake, a fear that stems from a sense of having no control. But this is ridiculous. You do have control over what you say and how you say it, so take the feeling one step further. Regard the audience as a gathering of your guests. Your opportunity to speak is their invitation to listen, so they are your guests. Here are three ways to do this.

1. *Adopt your "welcome persona."* When you invite people into your home, you show hospitality. You want people to feel at ease. So you offer amenities such as food and refreshments. As a presenter, you extend yourself. Imagine yourself shaking hands with every person in the audience as you might do if they really were guests in your home.

2. *Ensure comfort.* You want people to feel comfortable when you are speaking. Too often we assume the audience is our enemy and that we must keep them at a distance. Nonsense. You want them to pull them close to you so they see what kind of a presenter you are. You want to make them feel at ease as you speak.

3. *Remember that it's "your" house.* As a presenter, you own the stage. Your stage, as my colleague and performance coach Diana Theodores, Ph.D., says, is any area from which you present. That space may be the front of a room or the stage of a grand theater, or even from a seated position at a conference table. As the owner, you have a responsibility for your message as well as to those who are listening. Give them a good show by doing your best.

You control yourself, but you do not control everything. I still remember vividly the time I delivered a keynote presentation and my slides did not advance. The computer system froze. So I went to plan B; I pulled out my paper copy and continued. All was well until I set my folder down, only to knock over a glass of water on the podium. I can still see the stream of water flowing across the stage toward the power strip. "I am not an expert in electronics," I quipped to the audience as I fell to my knees to soak up the water with my handkerchief, "but I do know that water and electricity do not mix." I saved the system from shorting out, but I don't think I saved my presentation. It was fried!

When you seek to put others at ease, you are taking control of the situation. You are demonstrating a sense of confidence, and when you are feeling confident, you will feel a greater sense of control. You will adopt another persona: ownership of the message. You become the expert and you want to share your expertise with others. This is not arrogance; this is self-confidence.

ACTION STEPS

As you consider presenting:

- Visualize yourself in a place of relaxation, such as at home, at the beach, or in the mountains.

- Breathe in and out in a deep, rhythmic fashion.

- Imagine yourself radiating confidence as you stand up to speak.

Then ask . . .

- What can you do to make the audience feel more comfortable?

CHAPTER 4

STAND UP STRAIGHT
(AND DON'T FORGET TO BREATHE)

THE MAN AT THE PODIUM was tall and lanky. With his head tilted forward at an awkward angle he looked more like someone being hanged than someone reading a speech. Since this was a reading of a Senate amendment on C-SPAN, no one was really paying attention, but watching the Senate clerk labor through the text reminded me of occasions when I have seen executives stand at podiums with the same stance and demeanor: head down and plowing through the copy as if it were earth instead of prose.

Posture is so critical to public speaking. The stance of a speaker says much about how a speaker feels about what he is saying and how he wants the audience to receive his message. A speaker hunched over at the podium, or one who is furtively glancing sideways or upward but never at the audience, radiates discomfort. Rather than saying, "Hey, listen to me," the speaker's posture is saying, "Please don't look. I hate being up here."

Posture is something speech coaches work on with their presenters because posture is critical to delivery as well as to mood. Here are some ways proper posture can help you become a more effective speaker, either onstage with a podium or at the front of a room without one.

◆ *Stand tall.* Upright posture communicates respect for the audience. We stand up for people we respect, so by standing up you demonstrate your appreciation for listeners. Standing upright is also an indication of self-discipline; it says you are in control of yourself as well as of your message.

◆ *Get the right angle.* Ensure that you can stand straight. This is especially important if you are speaking from slides without benefit of a podium. Avoid slouching. If you are speaking from a podium, adjust the microphone to your height, even if you need to stand on a box to do so. (Note: Very tall people may find it challenging to adjust the microphone and in that instance it may be better to dispense with it and project your voice.)

◆ *Breathe regularly.* Singers are taught to breathe from the diaphragm, so an upright stance is important to getting air into the lungs and exhaling it as melody. Taking full breaths can also have a calming effect. Speakers who are nervous sometimes sound out of breath because they are; they are not taking in enough air to sustain both breath and words. So train yourself to breathe more deeply.

◆ *Look at the audience.* Make eye contact with people to whom you are speaking. If you are reading a speech, make a habit of looking up regularly, perhaps as often as every paragraph. Not only do you want to see the audience, you want them to see your face, which should radiate your energy.

◆ *Project your voice.* Stage actors are taught to be heard in the back row of a theater. Thanks to microphones, speakers are not so challenged, but they need to put energy into their voice. The voice is a speaker's instrument, so he or she must use it to convey words but also conviction.

These techniques are just that, techniques. While you can study them, they are useless until you practice them. And you don't need to wait for a formal occasion. Check your posture in a mirror. Look for ways to walk more upright, which, by the way, radiates confidence. Practice breathing from your diaphragm; it is good exercise too. Get in the habit of projecting energy in comments you make in staff meetings. No, you do not need to orate, but for items vital to you and your team you need to project passion for what you are saying.

James Lowther, Speaker of the British House of Commons early in the twentieth century, gave this advice: "There are three golden rules for Parliamentary speakers: Stand up. Speak up. Shut up."[1] The first two relate directly to posture, and the third relates to common sense. And that is something no speaker can project enough.

ACTION STEPS

As you consider delivering your next presentation, think about how a trusted colleague can help you:

- ◆ Make certain you stand up straight when you present.

- ◆ Project your voice so everyone can hear what you have to say.

- ◆ Ensure that you end your presentation in a timely fashion.

CHAPTER 5

LEAD YOUR PRESENTATION, DON'T HAVE IT LEAD YOU

❖

I am guessing you have heard this as an opening line for all too many PowerPoint presentations. Presenters use this line because either their slides are illegible or because they lack confidence in what they are presenting. In either case the presenter is doing the single worst thing any presenter can do: undercut her authority to deliver a message. Message development is the most important thing that any presenter, especially one who must lead others, can do.

Everyone likes to criticize PowerPoint as a presentation tool, but software is not the problem. The challenge is learning how to use it correctly so that you can present intelligibly and with confidence. Here are some tips you can use to create and deliver your next presentation.

- ◆ *Create.* Using presentation software to capture thinking is a wonderful tool. Jot ideas onto individual slides, and then after you have collected a number of them you can arrange and edit them into a flow you like.

- ◆ *Put meat on the bones.* Use the text function (Notes in PowerPoint) to write out your ideas in full sentences, even paragraphs. One criticism of PowerPoint is that it creates a form of shorthand thinking. If you write out your thoughts, you will think them through and organize them, and you will then be more prepared to deliver them.

◆ *Limit bullets.* Too many words on the slide risks illegibility. Use no more than five bullets per slide. A good test is to project your slides and then view them from the back of the room. If you can read them without trouble, you are likely okay. If not, trim the text.

◆ *Visualize.* We know that a picture is worth a thousand words. Utilize photographs and clip art to make your points. Charts, as long as they are clean and coherent, can do the same. Video, too, makes a wonderful addition to your presentation. And with the advent of low-cost video cameras and editing programs, video is a natural for inclusion. Remember, your audience would much prefer to look at pictures than read slides.

◆ *Deliver headlines.* The most common mistake presenters make is reading every slide word for word. Instead consider your slide as a launching point for the points you want to make. Each slide needs to have a key thought that either stands by itself or is amplified by a few tick points. No more.

◆ *Use handouts.* If you have a lot of data to deliver, give people handouts. You can reference the material on the screen and on the handout, but again keep the data points to a minimum. More data does not equate to more information; it leads to clutter.

◆ *Forget the rules.* There are no hard-and-fast rules about presentation save for this: be correct, be clear, and be convincing. So if you are comfortable reading your text as a speech, then do so. Invite a colleague to advance slides for you.

◆ *Let them remember you.* Entertainers always leave their audiences wanting more. You can do the same thing by ending with a story that summarizes or, better yet, captures the essence of what you have said. Create your story by quoting a customer or an employee, or by using an anecdote from the headlines or from history. Put some heart into your closing. People will remember you and what you have said.

One final rule for PowerPoint: As with alcohol, *use in moderation*. When leaders deliver a message, what matters most is what they say and how they say it. The message should be clear and concise and delivered with authority and conviction. PowerPoint can convey clarity, but it cannot convey passion. That comes from a presenter who looks at the audience as she delivers, utilizes her voice to demonstrate belief, and engages her body in the meaning of the moment.

For managers, making a presentation is an act of leadership. When you speak, you are representing the views of your organization either to stakeholders or to the public at large. You must come across as competent, knowledgeable, and professional. If PowerPoint can help you achieve this goal, use it. If not, then use the power of your leadership persona to connect with your audience in ways that demonstrate your ability to encourage others to follow your lead.[1]

ACTION STEPS

As you consider crafting your next PowerPoint presentation, think:

◆ Why do you think PowerPoint presentations fail?

◆   What do you want to include in your next PowerPoint
      presentation?

◆   What can you leave out of your next PowerPoint presentation?

◆   How will your next PowerPoint presentation have more impact?

CHAPTER 6

TURN POWERPOINT INTO
PERFORMANCE ART

❖

ONE OF THE CHALLENGES of presenting in PowerPoint—aside from the groans in the audience about one more slide presentation—is the dual task of creating content and delivering authenticity simultaneously.

While the slide may contain information, that is not your whole message; the total message is *what* you say and *how* you say it. This balancing act creates a dilemma that pulls at two distinct disciplines: creation and delivery.

You can simplify this dual challenge by preparing not only your message but also your delivery in advance. Here are five things to consider.

1. *Context.* When a presentation is created, it is good to keep the big picture in mind: Why am I giving this presentation? The reasons may be to provide a product overview or insights into an organizational transformation. Forgetting the big picture will cause the presenter to go off track. Focusing on the context sharpens the message.

2. *Segue.* Your presentation must flow evenly from slide to slide, so a presenter needs to develop links between the slides. Such links can be as simple as "As you saw in the previous slide, we have challenges. Now let me go into

detail on one of those challenges." The presenter is delivering a segue (a transition) that gives the audience a reason to pay attention.

3. *Headlines.* Every slide needs one; it carries the theme of the slide: cost, quality, or urgency. The words become what a presenter can punch up and deliver with emphasis. Pauses before and after a headline is spoken can be effective, but it is up to each presenter to deliver his or her own personal style.

4. *Specifics.* A good presenter balances content with reason. Too much content buries the meaning and the presentation dissolves into a litany of facts and figures. But shrewd presenters learn to focus on a specific item in slide, say a figure or a line on a graph, and tell a story about it. For example, a presenter might say, "If you focus on this trend line you see that as customers see our online videos, purchases go up." You make the words suit the picture.

5. *Delivery.* Most presenters fall into the trap of reading the words on the slide; a few others ignore the copy and say whatever comes into their heads. Neither is good. While a presenter should not typically read, there may be good reasons to read, perhaps if the bullets are short and tight or if there is a quotation. Then you use that headline as your basis of explanation.

There is an alternative: Script your message beforehand so you have a fully developed speaking text. Many senior executives have staff and speechwriters to do this for them, so it is not onerous for them, but for most others scripting out a full presentation is not always practical. It does have its virtues, however. It challenges you to put down precisely what you want to say so you can focus on delivery.

PowerPoint is a convenient whipping horse for failed presentations. It is true that this technology, and others like it such as Apple's Keynote, allows for the creation of elaborate graphics, data-laden charts, and even video, but that's not the real problem. The fault for poor presentations lies not with the technology but with the presenter.

The challenge is to focus on sharpening the message beforehand by focusing on what you will say and how you say it, so that when the time comes for you to deliver you are ready and raring to go . . . fully engaged to command the attention of your audience.[1]

ACTION STEPS

As you consider delivering your next PowerPoint presentation, think:

◆   What steps will you take to prepare your copy (what you will say out loud) in advance?

◆   How will you make certain your headlines complement your content?

◆   What will you do to make certain your segues tie into your theme?

CHAPTER 7

"TELL ME A STORY"

"EVEN THE PEOPLE who wrote the Bible were smart enough to know, 'tell them a story.' The issue was evil in the world; the story was Noah. . . . Now the Bible knew that and for some reason or another I latched on to that."[1]

That was Don Hewitt, creator and executive producer of one of the longest running shows in U.S. television history, *60 Minutes*, explaining the "secret" of his success. According to Steve Kroft, a *60 Minutes* correspondent, Hewitt did not concern himself with issues per se; he focused on stories shaped by those issues, be it war, consumer fraud, health investigations, or celebrity profiles.

Hewitt was fond of saying that every child realizes the importance of "tell me a story," but when we reach adulthood, we forget. Yet Hewitt's absolute commitment to story is something leaders, particularly those with big initiatives to push, should remember. Story is a form of person-to-person connection that leaders, as author and University of Pennsylvania Wharton School professor Stew Friedman writes, can use to connect with their followers.[2]

There are three reasons why a good story can be a useful leadership tool:

1. *To inform.* We all want the facts, but if a leader wants the facts to matter he needs to add a little seasoning. Stories

can take raw data and give them life. For example, why not use a spreadsheet to tell a story about rising sales or declining quality? Use the data to make your points. Then flesh out that explanation with stories about the effect on individuals, teams, and the company as a whole.

2. *To involve.* If you need to get people on your side, you need to involve them in the process. You need to engage their interest. For example, if an executive needs to persuade people to support an initiative, she can describe how the initiative will benefit the customer but also emphasize how it will improve the lot of employees too (more customers, more sales, more revenues, more jobs, more opportunities for promotion, etc.).

3. *To inspire.* Employees become jaded; there is only so much "importance" they can absorb, even when their jobs are at stake. So it falls to leaders to find ways to inspire their teams. Stories are the ideal vehicle for inspiring people because successful stories can dramatize the human condition. A story about a customer service representative who drove to the house of a customer to rectify an error, or a salesperson who drove through a raging blizzard to close a sale, can quickly become the stuff of corporate legend. These stories give sustenance in times of travail, and they say to an employee faced with long odds, "If she can do it, so can I."

There is another advantage to using stories, and that's something Hewitt alluded to with his reference to the Bible. Use stories to make your points rather than relying on platitudes. In fiction-writing workshops, they call this "Show, don't tell." For executives, this means avoiding corporate speak; instead, tell stories about how your initiatives will improve the lives of customers and employees.

Not every issue need be reduced to a story. There are times when a leader needs to be direct and to the point, to lay out the issue and the challenges in clear and precise language. For example, if a company is losing market share to a competitor, the sales manager might want to quantify the decline in sales by percentage and by lost revenue. Yet even in such circumstances, that same executive could drive the message home by naming the lost customers and describing the effect of their loss on the company.

A leader picks the right story at the right time to drive her point home, leaving no doubt about the importance of an initiative and its impact on the organization. It's up to a leader to use stories to dramatize urgency and humanize events so that listeners become followers.[3]

One final note: When you think of developing a story, do not overlook yourself or your organization. So advises a colleague of mine, Alisa Cohn, an executive coach based in the New York area. The personal story is useful when introducing yourself to a new team, when welcoming new employees, or when issuing a major challenge to the organization. Alisa suggests three story lines:

- One, who you are—or what your organization does

- Two, why I am here—or what our organization stands for

- Three, where we are going—together

ACTION STEPS

As you consider your next presentation, think:

- Why do people like stories so much?

- What memorable stories have you heard?

- What stories have inspired you?

CHAPTER 8

PROJECT OPTIMISM
THE RIGHT WAY

PEOPLE EXPECT THEIR LEADERS to be optimistic, and therefore every leader must integrate optimism into his or her communications. But such optimism must be tempered with reality.

"If you're cheerful, very optimistic . . . if you don't consider the possibility that you might have setbacks, then those setbacks are harder to deal with." That is Leslie R. Martin, coauthor with Howard S. Friedman (both Ph.D.s) of *The Longevity Project*, speaking to the *New York Times* about factors that facilitate long life spans.[1]

Dr. Martin's comments echo those of retired admiral James Stockdale, held prisoner for eight years by the North Vietnamese and the highest-ranking officer in the "Hanoi Hilton." While teaching at Stanford, author Jim Collins got to know Stockdale and one day he asked him about the POWs who did not return. Stockdale, who studied and wrote about Stoic philosophy, replied, "Oh, that's easy. The optimists."

Stockdale explained that the optimists kept hoping for release by Christmas. When Christmas came and went and they were not released, they hoped to get out by Easter. Over time, the repeated setbacks—as Dr. Martin would call them—became too much for them and "they died of a broken heart." Stockdale, as Collins describes in *Good to Great*, urged optimists to balance faith in the outcome with "the brutal facts of your current reality." Collins referred to this phenomenon as the Stockdale Paradox.[2]

Optimism therefore has its limits. And as much as leaders must radiate optimism, they must also keep their heads screwed on tight. They must balance optimism with current reality so that what they say and how they act reflects what is really happening.

Curiously, factors that do contribute to longer life, which are described in *The Longevity Project*, are "prudence and persistence."[3] Both are vital to leaders too. Leaders must make prudent decisions in every phase of management from recruitment and retention to resource allocation and strategic direction. Moreover, they must be persistent. Plans seldom go as defined; a leader must push for things to happen. That requires a degree of perseverance. Let me offer three tips to make optimism more real.

1. *Look on the bright side.* Work is tough (duh!). But that is no excuse for making work dull or challenges overwhelming. Take a cue from sports coaches. Their goals are wins and championships. They keep players focused on the possibilities, but they do not minimize the hard work required to attain those goals.

2. *Never overpromise.* Here is where reality enters the picture. You make certain you address the challenges the organization is facing. Be honest about the obstacles as well as what is required to get over or around them.

3. *Focus on what people do well.* People want to belong to an organization that makes them feel good about themselves. One way to deliver on that belief is to affirm what employees contribute. Note a job well done and thank them for their efforts.

When optimism is buttressed by prudence and persistence, it becomes more authentic. Therefore, people buy into it and feel better about what they are doing. The leader who projects this kind of optimism is believable and therefore more credible. What's more, we feel better about casting our lot with this individual. We want to believe in his or her leadership. Why? Because that leader makes us feel good about ourselves.

And who knows? While it may not extend our lives, it may extend our careers.

ACTION STEPS

As you consider projecting optimism, think:

- ◆ What two things will you do to convey optimism in your next presentation?

- ◆ What story do you want to tell that conveys optimism?

- ◆ What is the message of this story?

- ◆ How can you teach others to project optimism?

CHAPTER 9

MASTER THE ART OF
MEETING AND MINGLING

WATCHING THE FACE of the CEO talking to his employees was like watching a kid open presents on Christmas morning. The CEO was beaming as he listened to stories and dropped a few of his own. A bit earlier in the day I watched this same CEO come down from the stage where he was rehearsing a presentation and introduce himself to those in the room whom he had not yet met. This is a leader who knows how to work a room but does so with a touch of genuine humility. He is the kind of person who mingles easily and in the process gets people to talk about what is on their mind.

This executive has an ability to connect with others, and in doing so he opens the door to conversation. This conversation allows the senior leader to find out what is really going on in the organization, not just what the reports tell him. It is something every leader is capable of doing, but too many pass up the opportunity. Why? Because they feel they have too many other important things to do. But foolish is the leader who passes up a chance to meet and mingle with his people. Here are three ways to make certain it happens.

1. *Walk the halls.* An executive who stays in his office all day, day after day, is one who views the world from a spreadsheet, not from another human face. Walking the halls

gives the savvy executive a feel for the mood and tempo of the organization. You can feel the ups and downs in morale, as well as a sense of purpose.

2. *Eat in the cafeteria.* Is there anything more anachronistic than the executive dining room? This current recession may do some good after all. Kill the false sense of privilege that separates leaders from followers. Making yourself visible in the cafeteria is a great way to demonstrate solidarity.

3. *Hold office hours.* Okay, this may be a bit out of the ordinary, but if college professors can make themselves available to students, why can't executives hold open-door sessions with employees? CEOs in small organizations do this regularly, but I do know that many senior leaders in big companies regularly hold employee town hall meetings as well as appear regularly at small-group events. Web chats, too, are a good way to connect.

There is something else that comes from "meeting and mingling" and that is the opportunity to form a connection with others. That connection is reinforced with human interaction. It leads to support and eventually trust. It is the kind of support that gives a leader a boost when he or she needs to push hard on initiatives that may not be popular. Likewise, it gives the followers a sense of faith in their leader, a sense that the leader really cares about people as well as about the bottom line.

Never think you are too big to do this. James Glanz, a *New York Times* reporter, wrote about how his father, Irv (then a young TV sports anchor in Madison, Wisconsin) first met the legendary coach of the Green Bay Packers. At the close of the press conference, the coach climbed down from the podium, walked up to the young reporter, and stuck out his hand: "I'm Vince

Lombardi." No question that Vince wanted to make nice to a reporter, but also make no mistake that Lombardi was the kind of leader who knew how to connect with people.[1]

Do like Vince, and while they may not name a trophy in your honor, as the NFL did for Lombardi, those who matter most to your career—your colleagues—will respect you.

ACTION STEPS

As you consider ways to reach your people, think:

- What can I do to engage people in purposeful small talk?

- How much time should I spend engaging employees in conversation?

- How can I demonstrate better listening skills?

CHAPTER 10

LEVERAGE THE
ENERGY OF THE ROOM

THE AUDIENCE WAS on the edge of their seats and within moments broke into thunderous applause. The speaker had so moved the audience that some had tears in their eyes while others rose to their feet screaming with appreciation. At that moment the speaker and audience were in total harmony. All was bliss, unless you happened to be the next speaker.

This actually happened to a friend of mine, Bill Neale, coauthor of the Denison Organizational Culture Survey and an executive coach. Bill admitted that he did not rise to the challenge. But he learned from the experience and here's what he shared with me, along with additional tips I share with those I coach.

- *Read the moment.* Speakers must always acknowledge the reality of the moment. If the audience is cheering like mad for the person who preceded you, join in the applause. The worst you can do is stand there and pretend no one is clapping. Neale sometimes makes a point of summarizing what the previous speaker has said. Another technique is to pick something memorable from the previous act and use it in your presentation. Such references demonstrate your acknowledgment as well as your savvy.

- *Break the ice.* You need to find a way to connect with the audience. If the previous speaker was a big hit, comment on his performance. Or if the speaker bombed, compliment the effort. You may also make reference to what the audience is thinking or feeling at the moment, be it the weather, the economy, or the time of day. You must do something, anything, to break the ice so that attention shifts from *who you are* to *what you have to say.*

♦ *Know your stuff.* Repeated use of "ah," "um," "er" won't cut it on the stump. It is perfectly fine to script your presentation in advance. A strong, confident reading is far preferable to stumbling through a presentation that you are struggling to remember or, worse, trying to wing without notes. Such a performance does not inspire confidence in the audience, especially in any higher-ups who may be watching.

♦ *Keep it rolling.* The worst thing a speaker can do is drag out a presentation. So often, though, corporate speakers, as the saying goes, put "ten pounds of material into a one-pound bag." One way to shorten a presentation is to cut the "job justification." Relate the facts, not your career goals. Enhance them with anecdotes. And keep moving. Better a tight ten-minute presentation than a rambling twelve-minute opus.

Of course, the unexpected can always occur during a presentation. I recall the story of a comedian working a corporate gig in an outdoor tent. (Yes, you will find such entertainers.) He was fine with being outside in an open tent on a hot day without air-conditioning. He was okay with the din of loud traffic whizzing past a short distance behind him. But the final straw was when the buffet table was set up center stage right below his microphone. No speaker can compete with a hungry stomach.

CEOs always make certain they never follow a big-name act, be it a motivational speaker or an entertainer. But those farther down the hierarchy have no such luck; they must play the card the speaker organizer hands them.

Following a terrific presentation can set you up for success. As Bill Neale says, it gives you an opportunity to leverage the energy of the room. Standing up in front of a live audience requires practice. The more you do it, the better and more comfortable you are likely to become. Keep one key point in mind. The audience wants you to succeed. No one likes to see a speaker "die" onstage. So be cool, be brief, and keep smiling. You will do just fine.

ACTION STEPS

As you consider ways to leverage the energy of your presentation, think:

- How can I open big, such as with a story, a joke, or an acknowledgment of the audience?

- How can I focus on what people want to hear rather than what I want to say?

- How can I leave the audience wanting more of the message?

CHAPTER 11

AVOID NUANCE WHEN
YOU SPEAK OUT LOUD

I LOVE NUANCE.

The subtle unspoken communication between two people who know each other well. Good movie dramas are the stuff of nuance, a glance, a look of surprise, or a raised eyebrow. We know in an instant that the characters understand one another.

Never has this been more true than in actor Gary Oldman's portrayal of George Smiley, the protagonist of the 2011 film adaptation of *Tinker, Tailor, Soldier, Spy*. Oldman balances a brevity of words with a combination of straight head stares and a flickered eyebrow. Riveting stuff!

As effective as nuance may be in drama, it does not work as well for leaders. One leader who knew well how to drop nuance when he gave up the silver screen was President Ronald Reagan. When he visited the Berlin Wall in the mid-1980s, he said, "Mr. Gorbachev, tear down this wall." No nuance there.

We like it when our leaders provide clear direction. Certitude is something leaders must project, even when they may not be feeling it. But it's a leader's job to demonstrate that he or she understands the issues and can provide a path for others to follow. Clarity is essential when explaining a decision or a new course of action. Here are some suggestions for delivering it.

◆ *Show context.* Leaders need to frame issues so that people can understand them. That requires explaining what went into a decision and why it is important. It may be appropriate to recapitulate the debate that provoked discussion. People do want to know that their leader has thought about something before taking action. When explaining context, it is good to discuss outcome—what you expect to achieve. Outcome is the satisfaction of the goal.

◆ *Invite participation.* The people listening are the ones who will do the work. They will execute the decision. For that reason it may be appropriate to ask employees first. Employees are hired to do the work, but if an employer wants more than compliance, he or she needs to allow employees to have a say in how the work is done. The invitation to participate demonstrates that the boss views employees as contributors.

◆ *Be specific.* Nuance is the enemy of specificity. When asking employees to do something, be clear and direct about what you want to achieve. The period of explanation is over; now is the time for action. "Link actions to goals. Do this and we will reduce costs. Do that and we will improve quality. Do both things and we will have happy customers." Employees in turn will figure out the action steps that enable the fulfillment of the goals.

Clarity does not rule out deliberation. Not only should leaders think before they speak, they should consider alternatives before asking their followers to undertake a bold initiative. When weighing options, nuance plays a very different role. Seldom are issues cast as either-or options; there are always trade-offs. Understanding nuance, as in what the consequences are and what the impact individuals have, is a good way to parse the issue.

For example, in a human resources department that wants to position its company as an employer of choice, its executive team needs to consider how it recruits, develops, and retains employees and what kind of investment is necessary to do so. Will that investment pay off in attracting more capable employees? Can the company afford to keep them or will they be recruited away?

The decision will require debate and deliberation, but that debate need not be carried out in public. The to-ing and fro-ing can occur behind closed doors, and when the decision is made it must be communicated in a straightforward manner.

People may remember dramas where characters and dialogue are nuanced, but they do not follow leaders who are.

ACTION STEPS

As you consider ways to make certain people understand what you are saying, think:

- ◆ What can I do to be specific and provide actions steps to make certain my meaning is clear?

- ◆ How can I enunciate and use simple language to make sure I speak more clearly?

- ◆ What questions can I ask to ensure that people understand the message?

CHAPTER 12

DEVELOP YOUR
LEADERSHIP PRESENTATION

ONE OF YOUR principal duties as a leader will be to deliver speeches. Here's a handy guide to developing a speech.

- ◆ *Consider context.* Leaders address issues. It is not enough to tell an audience what they want to hear. You must tell them what they must hear. That is, employees may want to learn about bonus compensation, but first you *must* establish the criteria for achieving the bonus. The rewards may be sweet but qualifying for them may be challenging. Honest leaders lay out the details.

- ◆ *Focus your thoughts.* What do you want to say? Sum up your message in one hundred words by considering what you would like the audience to think about or do after they hear your presentation. Make this message the foundation for your entire presentation.

- ◆ *Research your topic.* Find out what other people think about your idea. Others include members of your team or the leaders of your organization. Also, read about your topic in your newspaper, trade journals, or books. The web can also be a terrific resource; check out the newspaper websites. Many allow you to download articles free of charge.

◆ *Outline your thoughts*. Put things down on paper. Make notes and string them together; then organize them. You can use sticky notes, index cards, or full sheets. The point is to put your thoughts on paper. If you use notes or cards you can shuffle the order to find the right flow.

◆ *Find stories*. There's an old saying in journalism: Names make news, people make pictures. That is especially true for stories! All of us love hearing stories. The stories can be about people in your organization or people in the news or people from history. Use stories as seasoning for the stew. They add flavor and spice. Best of all, people remember stories; it just may be the best way to get your message across. (Hint: Humor is fine too. Just keep it clean as well as upbeat. Avoid jokes at the expense of others—except yourself!)

◆ *Draft your words*. Write your thoughts down. Don't be intimidated by the blank screen. Begin by rekeying your outline, and pretty soon you'll be on your way.

◆ *Show it to colleagues*. Get someone you trust to read the draft. Ask that person if the speech sounds like you and makes the points clearly and succinctly.

◆ *Rewrite*. Writing is rewriting. From William Shakespeare to Tom Clancy, every writer rewrites to make the points clearer.

◆ *Rehearse*. Yup. Say the speech out loud in front of a mirror. Don't be afraid. Many famous people, including Winston Churchill, did this regularly. The more you rehearse the more comfortable you will be with the words and the word order and with the emphasis each word, each phrase, and each sentence needs.

ACTION STEPS

As you compose your next presentation, think:

- ◆ What does the audience want to hear?

- ◆ What do they need to hear?

- ◆ How will I make the business case for my presentation?

- ◆ What stories might I relate?

HANDBOOK ON COMMUNICATING LEADERSHIP PRESENCE

STEP 1
POWER PRESENCE: BASIC TIPS

◆ When you meet someone for the first time, make eye contact. Give a firm handshake. (Note: This behavior is considered rude in certain Asian cultures. Be mindful and respectful of the customs of your management counterparts.)

◆ If you are the host, be courteous. Offer coffee or refreshments.

◆ If you are a guest, compliment the host on his office.

◆ Smile when new people enter the room.

◆ Maintain an erect carriage when you walk and when you speak to people.

STEP 2
WHEN SPEAKING AS A LEADER . . .

◆ Think about what you want to say and why. Itemize benefits and roadblocks. Consider how you will overcome the roadblocks.

◆ Develop your "elevator speech" for every single key issue.

◆ Present your ideas clearly and coherently.

◆ Rehearse your talking points.

◆ Think of stories to augment your points.

◆ Ask people for their ideas.

◆ If you are the team leader, do not be the first one to voice an opinion. It will color all the others.

◆ Invite people to support your ideas.

◆ Project optimism.

◆ Radiate hope.

◆ Smile. It invites people to share their ideas with you.

When leading a meeting . . .

◆ Smile when you enter the room. Shake hands with everyone.

◆ Engage in small talk until everyone gets settled. Focus on speaking with people you don't see much.

◆ Call the meeting to order promptly.

◆ Overview the agenda quickly. Promise to end the meeting early, if possible.

- Roll through the topics.

- Facilitate the discussion by keeping people on point. Eliminate cross talk.

- If resolution cannot be achieved, or if more discussion is necessary, take the topic offline and move on.

- Solicit participation from everyone.

- Summarize key points and roll on.

- Make a meaningful summary, providing action steps if appropriate.

[**Hint:** It is good practice to share the chair. That is, invite other people to set the agenda and chair the meeting. This does two things: It enables you to participate more in the conversation and it allows the people on your team to develop their own leadership capacity.]

When "pitching across borders" . . .

Before the meeting:

- Have coffee or lunch with your colleagues.

- Explain your issues and why you need their support.

- Identify their objections.

- Identify your allies as well as your adversaries.

- Invite your allies to help you win over (or neutralize) your adversaries.

- Commit to finding mutually beneficial solutions.

During the meeting:

- Arrive early and greet people as they arrive. Engage in small talk. Keep it light. Smile if you like.

- Call the meeting to order. Promise to be brief.

- Summarize your purpose with a story illustrating why this is important.

- Top line your topics. Be sure to mention objections.

- Share the meeting with your allies. Get them active in your pitch process.

- Identify roadblocks as well.

- Solicit ideas from your adversaries. Demonstrate empathy. Be flexible. Strive for mutual benefit.

- Look for things to "give up" so that your adversary looks good. Credit your adversaries for their "wins."

- Ask for commitments.

- Counter objections with solutions.

- Keep the discussion moving.

- Schedule the next meeting.

When "pitching up" . . .

- Enter the room with confidence. Tell yourself that you know your subject better than anyone else does.

- Smile at everyone in the room and shake hands if appropriate.

- Make a comment about the day, addressing things like the weather, sports, traffic, etc.

- Reconfirm the amount of time you have. Meetings often run behind, so you want to determine your time.

- Summarize in thirty seconds what you will say. Promise that you will end early; they will love you for it.

- Tell a story about what you are about to say.

- Launch into your story—tell them what you are going to tell them, tell them, and then tell them again.

- Make a concluding statement.

- Invite questions.

- Thank the group and smile as you exit.

When giving a speech . . .

Before you take the stage:

- Close your eyes. Think of a place where you like to relax, such as the beach, the mountains, your favorite easy chair.

- Breathe deeply for one full minute.

- Rotate your head from side to side, gently stretching your neck muscles.

- Relax your facial muscles.

- Think about your message. Remind yourself that you know your stuff.

As you take the stage:

- Walk to the center of the room (or podium) with assurance.

- Smile as you walk.

◆ When you reach the podium or the center of the room, stand up straight.

◆ Look to the front of the room, then the back and from side to side. Nod and acknowledge the applause.

As you begin your presentation:

◆ Smile all around as you take a deep breath.

◆ Acknowledge your introduction.

◆ Comment on something topical, such as what previous speakers have said, the situation, or even the weather.

◆ Deliver the hook of your presentation, why you are speaking today.

During your presentation:

◆ Punctuate key points by raising your voice.

◆ Assume a neutral but authoritative tone as you deliver your presentation.

◆ Use appropriate gestures. You may punctuate key points with hand gestures. Reveal your hand in profile, not the open palm.

◆ Shift your eye contact from side to side and front to back.

◆ Pause for emphasis. Hold the pause for dramatic effect.

◆ If you are not at a podium, stroll the stage. Do not pace. Walk slowly to one side and deliver a portion of your presentation. Walk to the other side of the stage and deliver more of the presentation. Move to the center of the stage and deliver still more. Do not say something crucial as you walk.

- Look to the audience when you make a key point. Hold the moment; then explain your key point.

As you conclude your presentation:

- Summarize your key points.

- Include a call to action, if desired.

- Close with a story.

- Thank the audience for listening.

- Acknowledge the applause with a polite nod.

As you take questions:

- Smile at the audience. Relax your posture a bit. Open your stance. This shows that you are inviting people to ask you something.

- Acknowledge questioners. Restate questions so the entire audience can hear.

- After you answer, check for understanding. Ask if the question has been answered.

Handling objections:

- Acknowledge the tough question. Say something like, "That is a tough question and it deserves a good answer."

- Remain calm. Breathe deeply. Smile before answering.

- Do not be afraid to say you don't know. Promise to deliver an answer at a later date.

- Always state the truth. Always.

STEP 3
WHEN LISTENING AS A LEADER . . .

◆ Look at people when they are speaking to you. Make eye contact.

◆ Ask open-ended questions, such as "Tell me about . . ." or "Could you explain this?"

◆ Consider the "what if" question: "What if we looked at the situation like this?"

◆ Leverage the "why" question: "Why do we do it this way?"

◆ Employ the "how" question: "How can you do this?"

STEP 4
WHEN LEARNING AS A LEADER . . .

◆ Reflect on what people have told you.

◆ Think about what you have not observed. Are people holding back? If so, why?

◆ Consider how you can implement what you have observed.

◆ Get back to people who have suggested ideas to you and thank them.

◆ Look for opportunities to collaborate with others.

STEP 5
WHEN PERSUADING THE UNPERSUADED . . .

◆ Pay attention to the situation. Identify the factors that are influencing individuals as well as the group as a whole.

- Find common ground. Determine what people agree on and why they agree.

- Demonstrate inclusiveness. Make it known that everyone and their ideas are welcome.

- Turn the opposition's strength into its greatest weakness. Consider what is or may be the flaw in your opponent's argument. Explore it and turn it to your benefit. Craft your argument around the virtues of small vs. big, custom vs. mass-made, local vs. global, or individual vs. corporate.

- Give people a stake in the outcome. Demonstrate how people will benefit by accepting the new way of doing things.

- Invite some people to leave. Unity demands agreement and compromise. Those who cannot come together should be asked to leave the team.

- Build consensus with the team.

NOTES

Chapter 2: Present as a Leader

1. First published as "Lead with Presence," in WABC Coaches eZine, February 2009. Used with permission.

Chapter 4: Stand Up Straight (and Don't Forget to Breathe)

1. http://en.wikipedia.org/wiki/James_Lowther,_1st_Viscount_Ullswater.

Chapter 5: Lead Your Presentation, Don't Have It Lead You

1. http://blogs.harvardbusiness.org/baldoni/2009/04/five_things_leaders_can_do_to.html.

Chapter 6: Turn PowerPoint into Performance Art

1. First published as "The PowerPoint Balancing Act," *Bloomberg/Businessweek*, August 3, 2010. Used with permission.

Chapter 7: "Tell Me a Story"

1. Steve Kroft, "Don Hewitt's Success Secret," *60 Minutes*, August 23, 2009.

2. Stew Friedman, "How a 2 Minute Story Helps You Lead," *Harvard Business Review* (HBR.org), August 4, 2009.

3. First published as "Why Leaders Need to Use Stories: A Lesson from Don Hewitt," *Harvard Business Review* (HBR.org), August 25, 2009. Used with permission.

Chapter 8: Project Optimism the Right Way

1. Katherine Bouton, "Eighty Years Along a Longevity Project Still Has Ground to Cover," *New York Times*, April 18, 2011.

2. Jim Collins, *Good to Great* (New York: Harper Business, 2001), pp. 83–87. Additional information on the Stockdale Paradox was based upon information on Jim Collins's website, http://www.jimcollins.com/media_topics/brutal-facts.html.

3. Howard S. Friedman, Ph.D., and Leslie R. Martin, Ph.D., *The Longevity Project* (New York: Hudson Street Press, 2011).

Chapter 9: Master the Art of Meeting and Mingling

1. James Glanz, "Watching Favre from Baghdad Evokes Memories," *New York Times,* December 17, 2008, http://www.nytimes.com/2008/12/17/sports/football/17glanz.html.

INDEX

ABOUT THE AUTHOR

John Baldoni is the president of Baldoni Consulting LLC, a full-service executive coaching and leadership development firm. He is an internationally recognized leadership educator, executive coach, and author of a dozen books, including *Lead with Purpose*, *Lead Your Boss*, and *The Leader's Pocket Guide*. John speaks throughout North America and Europe, and in 2012 Leadership Gurus International ranked him No. 10 on its list of global leadership experts. John has authored more than 400 leadership columns for a variety of online publications, including *CBS MoneyWatch*, *Harvard Business Review*, *Forbes*, *The Washington Post*, and *Inc*. His leadership resource website is www.johnbaldoni.com.